Learning About Your State and Community

PEARSON
Scott Foresman

Editorial Offices: Glenview, Illinois • Parsippany, New Jersey • New York, New York
Sales Offices: Parsippany, New Jersey • Duluth, Georgia • Glenview, Illinois • Coppell, Texas • Ontario, California • Mesa, Arizona

www.sfsocialstudies.com

ISBN 0-328-05535-2

Copyright © Pearson Education, Inc.
All rights reserved. Printed in the United States of America. The blackline masters in this publication are designed for use with appropriate equipment to reproduce copies for classroom use only. Scott Foresman grants permission to classroom teachers to reproduce from these masters.

7 8 9 10-V034-12 11 10 09 08 07

Contents

Learning About Your State and Community

Contents

To the Teacher	iv
The United States	1
The Region Where We Live	2
The Land in Our State	3
Bodies of Water	4
Weather	5
Natural Resources	6
Resources and Industries	7
Plants and Animals	8
State History	9
Early People in Our State	10
Early Explorers	11
Life for Early Settlers	12
Historical Places	13
Famous People	14
Where People Live	15
Changes in Population	16
What People Do	17
Then and Now	18
State People in National Government	19
Who Governs Our State?	20
The Governor of Our State	21
The State Legislature	22
The Judicial Branch	23
Education	24
Industries and the Economy	25
State Celebrations	26
Cultural Resources	27
Arts and Crafts	28
Literature	29
Sports	30
Getting Around Our State	31
Places to Visit	32
Something to Write Home About	33
State Symbols	34
Cities and Towns	35
Make a Map of Your Community	36
Your Local Government	37
Getting the Help You Need	38
Important People from Your Community	39
Touring Your Town or City	40
Community Landmark	41
Your Community: Past and Future	42
Our State and Your Community at a Glance	43
Community Hero	44

To the Teacher

This book helps reinforce and expand students' knowledge about their state and community. It covers the key social studies strands of citizenship, culture, economics, geography, history, and science and technology. Students can use the exercises individually, in pairs, or in small groups.

A variety of approaches to learning is used throughout *Learning About Your State and Community.* Some exercises contain fill in the blank. Others require short answer. Sometimes students are asked to create a finished product such as a new state logo or advertising brochure. Responses on some pages are open ended. Whenever possible, encourage students to be creative in their responses.

Other exercises direct students to do research. Suggested research resources include the library, the encyclopedia, maps, and the Internet. As you begin, you may want to incorporate a lesson on how to do research by discussing and demonstrating how to use the library and how to find pertinent information in an encyclopedia, the Internet, or other resource. Periodic review of these skills helps students become familiar with the resources they use. It also helps them practice their research skills.

Learning About Your State and Community helps students better understand the place where they live. As they work through the book, they integrate what they know and what they learn. It also helps you evaluate students' comprehension and application of what they have learned.

Name _____ Date _____

The United States

There are 50 states in the United States of America. Use two-letter abbreviations to label each state on the map below. Then draw a ★ and label the capital of our state.

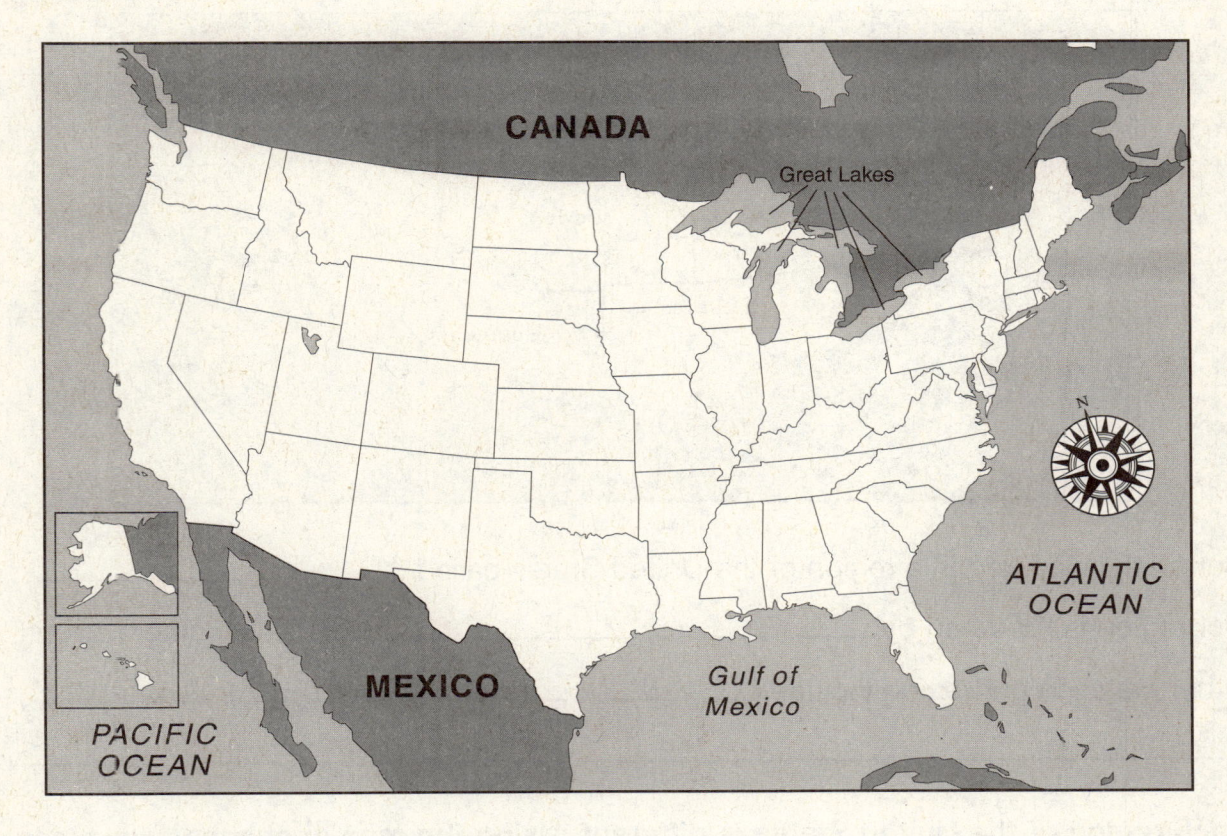

Do you know our neighbors? Write the state, country, or body of water that answers each question below. There may be more than one answer.

What lies to the north of our state? _____
_____

What lies to the west of our state? _____
_____

What lies to the east of our state? _____
_____

What lies to the south of our state? _____
_____

© Scott Foresman

Learning About Your State and Community

1

Name _____ Date _____

The Region Where We Live

The map shows the five main regions of the United States. Find our state and shade it with a pencil or pen. Then use the map to complete the sentences.

Our state is located in a region of the United States called _____.

Our region is bordered by _____ other regions.

Other states in our region include _____

_____.

Each region of the United States is different. Using the map above, answer these questions about the regions of the United States.

Which two regions are bordered in part by the Great Lakes? _____

_____

Which is the only region not bordered by an ocean or gulf? _____

Which is the only region not bordered by another country? _____

2   Learning About Your State and Community

Name _____   Date _____

The Land in Our State

When you think of our state, do you think of mountains, deserts, hills, forests, plains, or plateaus? In the space below, draw and label the landforms and vegetation that are most common in our state.

Use resources you have found to learn more about our state's land. What three facts do you find the most interesting? Write them below.

_____
_____
_____
_____
_____
_____

Learning About Your State and Community

Name _____ Date _____

Bodies of Water

When you travel around our state, do you pass by a river or a lake? What bodies of water, if any, are near where you live? In the space below, trace or draw an outline of our state. Locate your city or town and then draw in the main bodies of water. Color the bodies of water blue and label them.

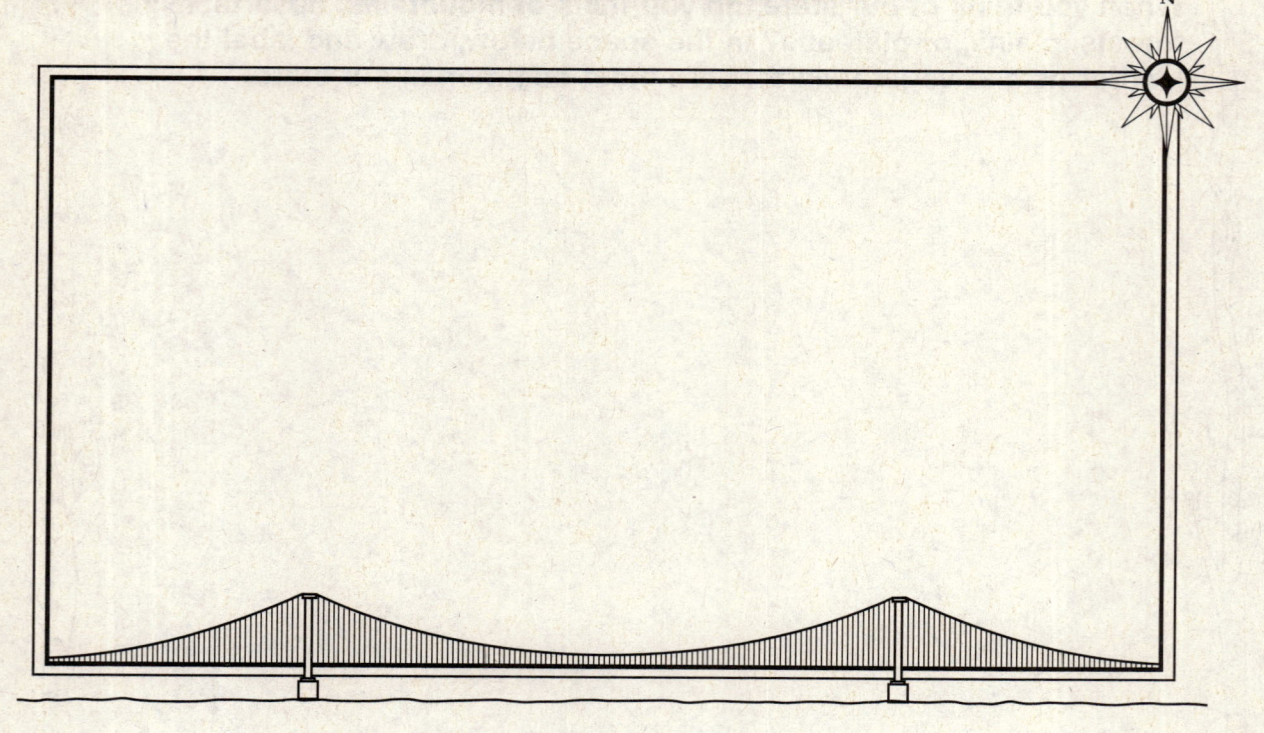

Write one or two sentences about the bodies of water in our state. If necessary, use an encyclopedia or other resources.

_____
_____
_____
_____
_____
_____
_____

Learning About Your State and Community

Name _____ Date _____

Weather

Weather is the day-by-day change in temperature and rainfall. How cool or how warm is our state at different times of the year? Use an almanac as a resource to complete a line graph.

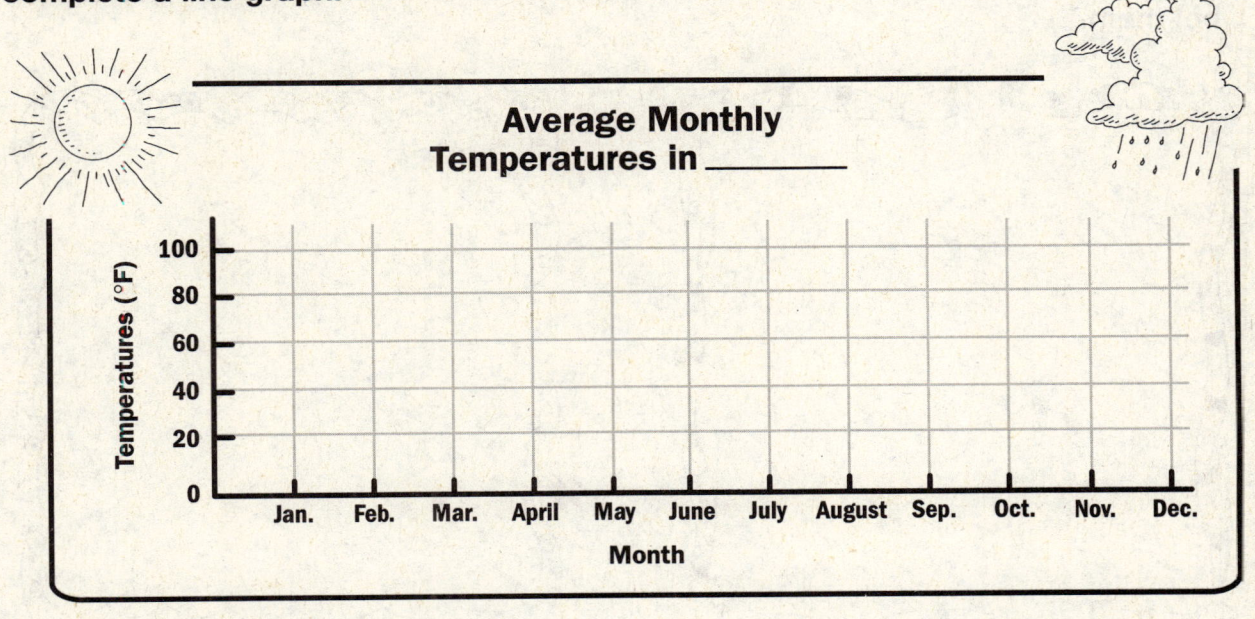

Average Monthly Temperatures in _____

(Graph: Temperatures (°F) from 0 to 100 on y-axis; Months Jan., Feb., Mar., April, May, June, July, August, Sep., Oct., Nov., Dec. on x-axis)

Month

Give additional facts about the weather in our state.

1. The record high temperature is _____. It happened on _____ _____ _____ in _____.
   (month) (day) (year)   (city)

2. The record low temperature is _____. It happened on _____ _____ _____ in _____.
   (month) (day) (year)   (city)

3. The average annual rainfall is _____.

4. Some types of storms we see are _____.

5. I remember one storm when _____
   _____.

Learning About Your State and Community

5

Name _____ Date _____

Natural Resources

Many states celebrate some of their natural resources through state symbols. Use an encyclopedia, Internet search, or almanac to identify our state's symbols. Choose two symbols of our state. Draw a picture of each in the space below and label them.

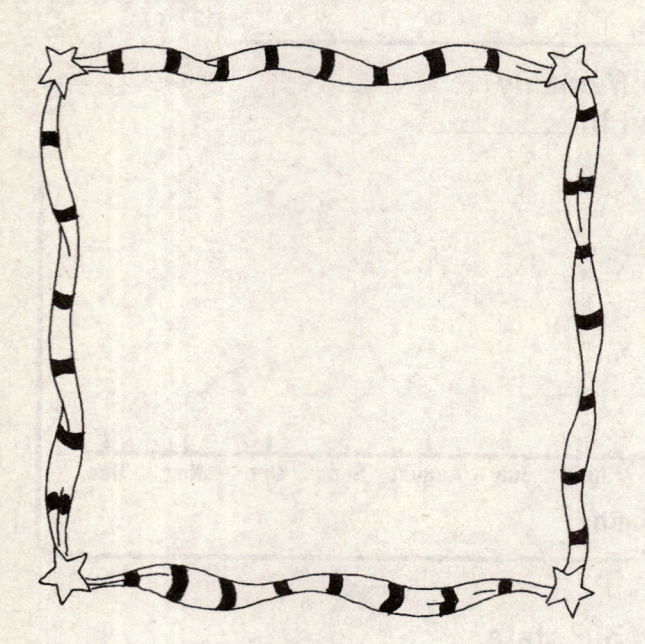

Use an encyclopedia, your social studies book, or resources from the library to learn about the natural resources in our state. Write a sentence to answer each question.

How do the people in our state benefit from water resources? _____
_____

What underground resources are important to our state? Explain why each resource is

important. _____
_____

6   Learning About Your State and Community

Name _____   Date _____

Resources and Industries

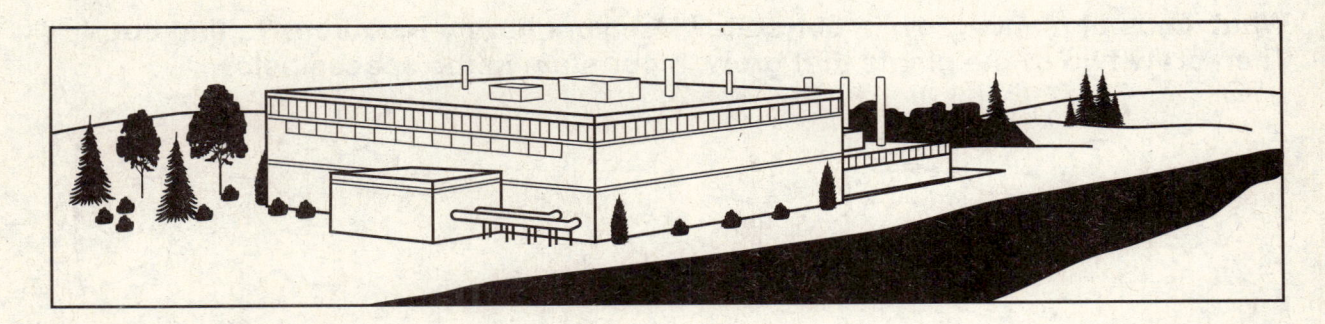

Find out what industries use the natural resources in our state. Write a class letter to at least three different companies that represent the industries in our state. Ask the following questions.

1. What industry is your company a part of?
2. What natural resources does your company use the most?
3. What do you use the natural resources for?

Use the answers to your questions to complete the chart below.

Industry	Name of Company	Natural Resources Used	How Each Resource Is Used

Learning About Your State and Community

Name _____ Date _____

Plants and Animals

What kinds of plants grow in our state? Use your library resources to find out. Then draw two of the plants that grow in our state in the spaces below.

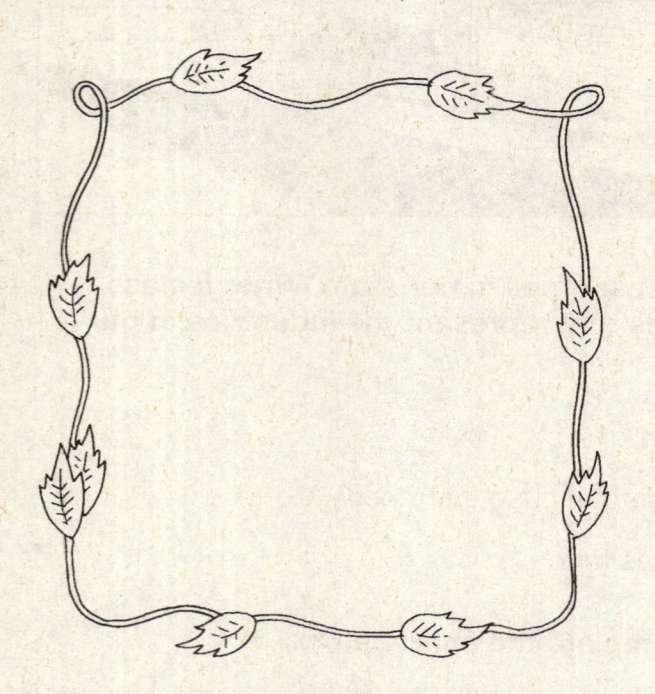

Many different kinds of wild animals live in our state. Use what you know to draw in the space below two of the animals that live in our state. Describe the habitat of each animal.

8

LEARNING ABOUT YOUR STATE AND COMMUNITY

Name _____ Date _____

State History

Our state has an interesting history. Use the resources you have in your library or elsewhere to complete the sentences.

_____ became a state in the year _____. It was the _____ state to join the United States. One important person in our state's history is _____. This person is important because _____. Before our region was a state, an important event that happened in its history was _____ _____. After statehood, one important event that happened here was _____ _____. In my opinion, the most interesting event in our state's history was _____ _____. I think this event is interesting because _____ _____.

Suppose that you are witnessing an important event in our state's history. On the back of this page, write two or three sentences that describe the event. Then tell why you think it was important. Draw a picture to illustrate your description.

© Scott Foresman

Learning About Your State and Community

9

Name _____ Date _____

Early People in Our State

People have lived in our state for a long time. Historians use resources, such as artifacts, to find out about these early people. Use library or Internet resources to complete the following graphic organizer. Write the name of the earliest inhabitants we know about in our state in the middle circle. In the other circles, write facts such as the homes they lived in, the way they gathered their food, tools they used, and what they wore.

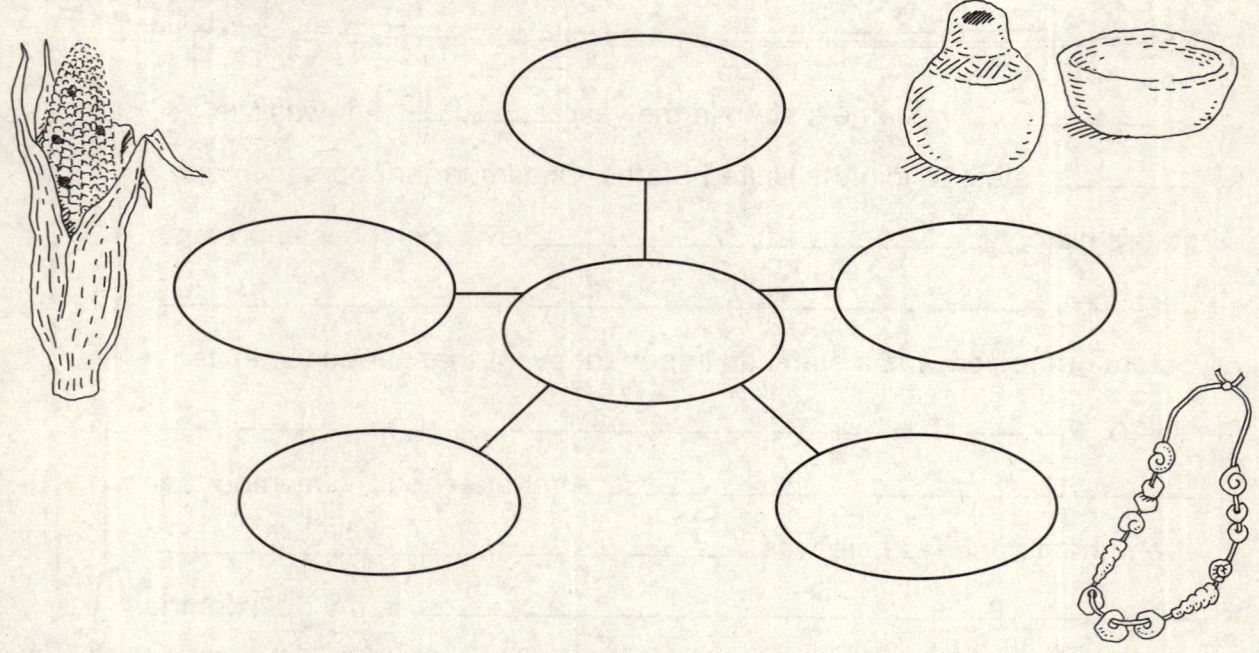

In the past, people may have called some of our cities and towns by different names. Find up to three cities or towns in our state that had different names. Use resources such as your library or the Internet. Put the information in the chart below.

Name of City or Town Today	Name in the Past

10 Learning About Your State and Community

Name _____ Date _____

Early Explorers

Explorers from other parts of the world or the early United States probably came to our state a long time ago. Where did they come from? Who did they find here when they came? Research to learn more and then complete the following summary.

Explorers from _____ came

first to what is now known as the state of _____

in the year _____. They met a group of native

people called the _____. The settlers

who came after the explorers ended up mainly in places such as

_____ and _____.

Most of the new settlers made their living by

_____.

Name one of the early explorers or settlers who came to our state. Use a resource such as the library to find out about the person. Tell the person's story in two or three sentences.

_____

_____

_____

_____

Learning About Your State and Community

Name _____ Date _____

Life for Early Settlers

Use an encyclopedia, Internet research, or a book about our state to complete the diagram below. Write details that support the idea that early settlers in our state, who came after the explorers, had to work hard to survive.

Main Idea: Many of the early settlers worked hard to survive.

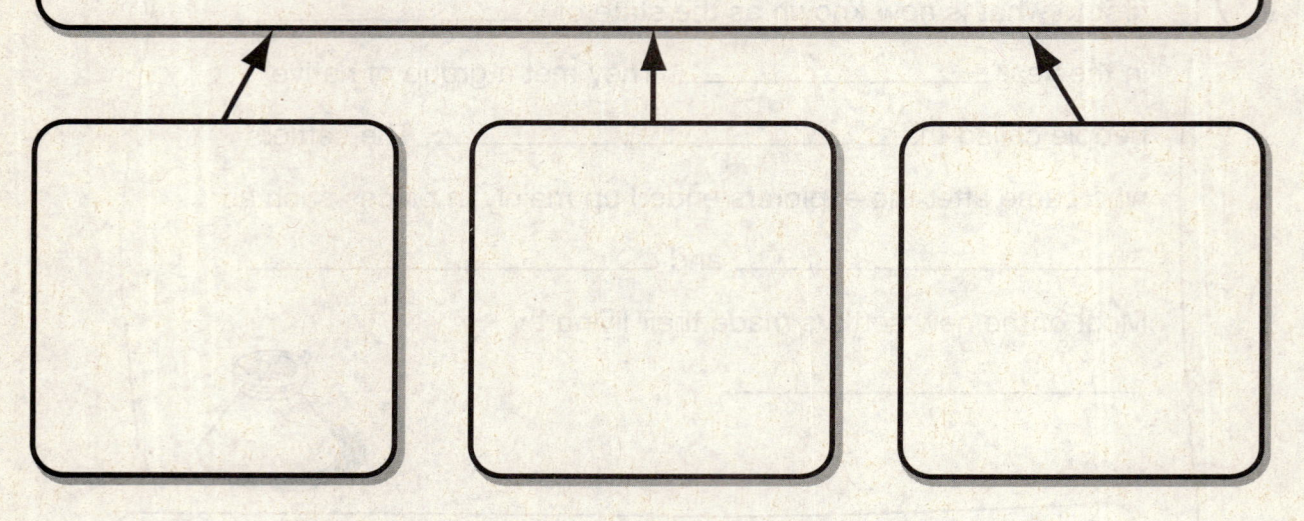

Suppose that you were one of the early settlers in our state. What were your chores? Draw a picture of one of your chores. Then next to your picture write a caption that explains what your picture shows.

Caption: _____

_____

_____

_____

_____

_____

_____

_____

Name _____ Date _____

Historical Places

Our state has many historical places. List three of the most famous historical landmarks in our state. Then tell where each landmark is and why it is important in our state's history. Draw a picture of the one you like best.

Historical Landmark	Where the Landmark Is Located	Why the Landmark Is Important

Encourage tourists to visit a historical landmark in our state. In the space below, create an advertisement for the site.

Learning About Your State and Community

13

Name _____ Date _____

Famous People

Who has contributed greatly to the history of our state? Fill in the picture frames with drawings of these famous people you have copied from books or the Internet. Write a caption for each picture that tells who the person was and how he or she helped make our state what it is today.

_____ _____ _____
_____ _____ _____
_____ _____ _____
_____ _____ _____
_____ _____ _____

If you could interview one of the people above, what would you ask that person about what he or she did? Write the question and how you think your subject would respond on the back of this page.

14   Learning About Your State and Community

Name _____ Date _____

Where People Live

Many conditions affect where people live in a state. Landforms and natural resources often determine the areas where people settle in large numbers. Find a map of population density for our state in an encyclopedia, Internet research, or book of our state's history; this shows where the most people in our state live. Copy that map in the space below. Also copy the map's key.

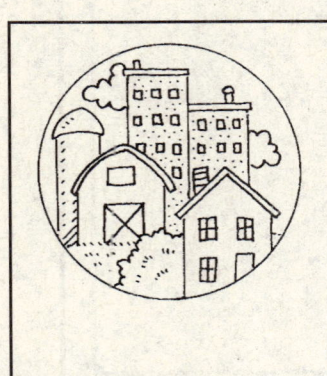

Population per Square Mile

People per Square Mile

Use your map to write a general statement about the population of our state.

_____
_____
_____

Learning About Your State and Community

15

Name _____   Date _____

Changes in Population

Population in our state is always changing. Use sources such as an encyclopedia or an almanac to help you complete the table.

Year	Population	10-Year Change
1950		////////////////
1960		
1970		
1980		
1990		
2000		

Use the information above to plot a line graph. Write the lowest population number on the blank line at the bottom left side of the grid. Write the highest number at the top. Fill in the in-between levels with equal population totals. Place dots above each 10-year mark to show the number of people. Connect the dots when you are finished.

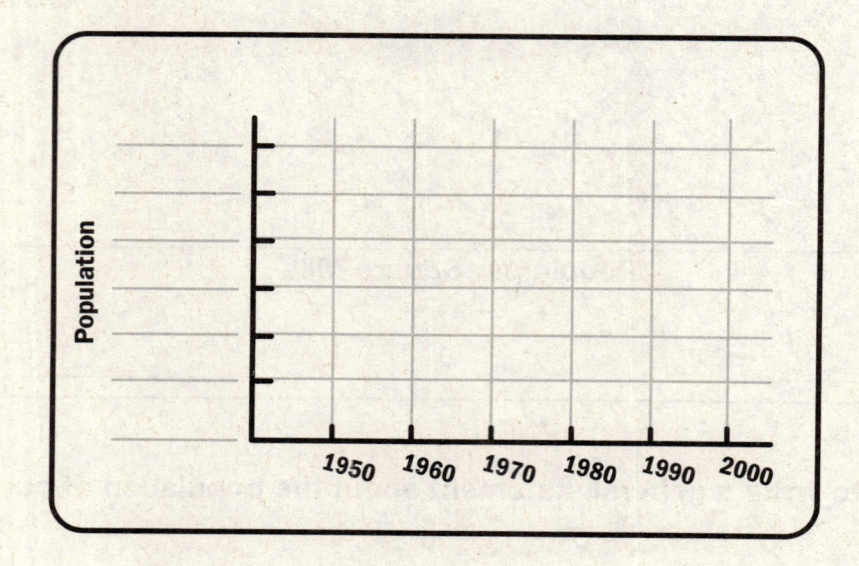

16

Learning About Your State and Community

Name _____ Date _____

What People Do

What kinds of work do people in our state do? Use a book about our state or research our state government's Web site on the Internet to complete the table below.

Jobs for People in _____

Industry	Types of Jobs
Farming	
Manufacturing	
Construction	
Health Care	
Tourism	
Government Services	

Choose one of the jobs above that interests you. Write a short paragraph on why you are interested in the job. Also write about what training a person needs, such as college or trade school, to get into that job field.

_____
_____
_____
_____
_____
_____
_____
_____

Learning About Your State and Community

17

Name _____ Date _____

Then and Now

Use what you have learned about our state's history to compare the past and the present. What was our state like in the past? Put your answers in the Past circle. What is our state like now? Put your answers in the Present circle. How was our state the same in the past as it is in the present? Put your answers in the section labeled Both.

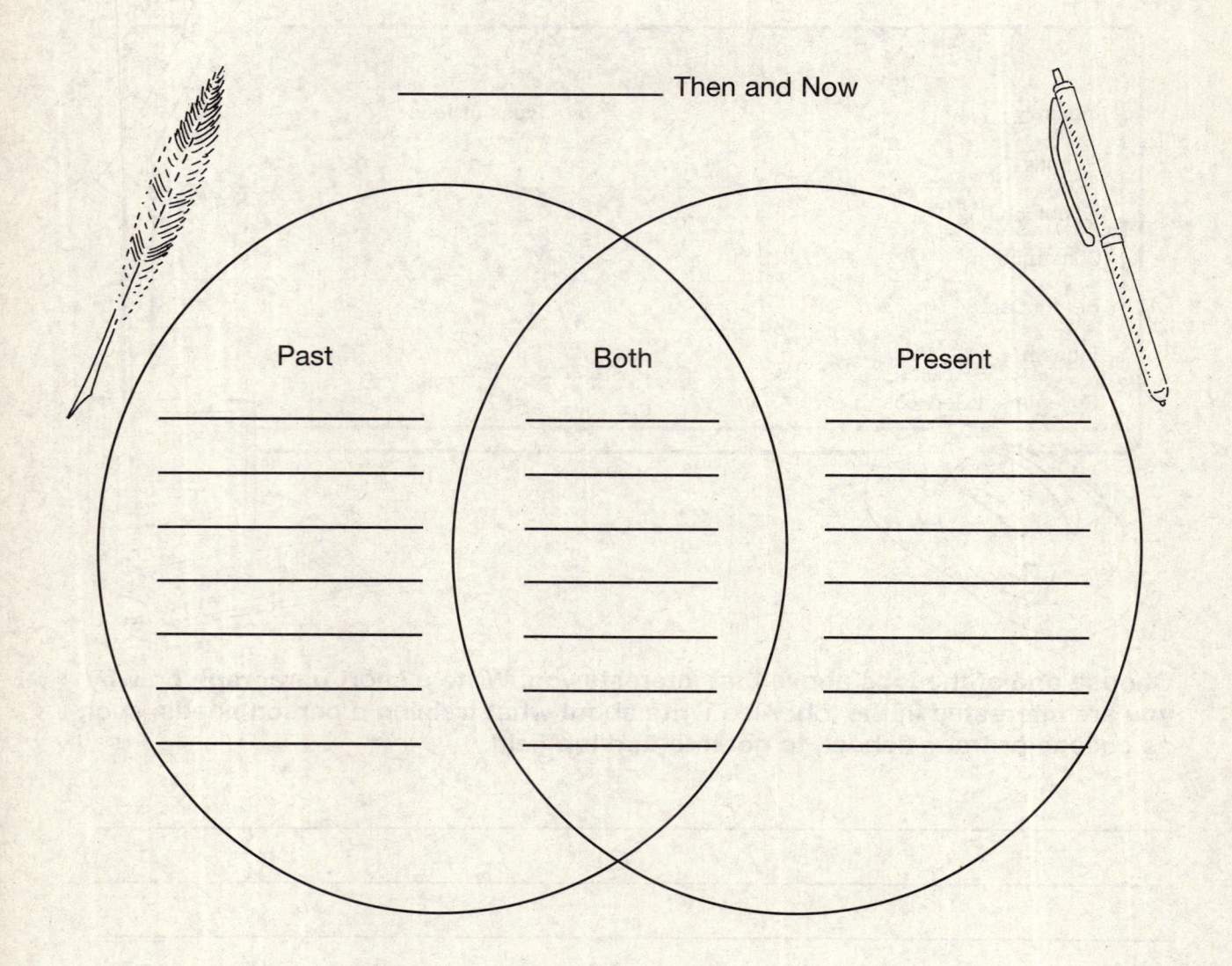

_____ Then and Now

Past   Both   Present

Write a short news story about the biggest change that you think has happened in our state. Write your story on the back of this page.

18   Learning About Your State and Community

Name _____ Date _____

State People in National Government

Who from our state has served or is currently serving in the national government of the United States? Put each person's name in the correct space. If necessary, use the back of this page to write more names. If no one from our state has served in the Executive or Judicial Branches, leave the space blank.

The United States Government

- Executive Branch
- Judicial Branch
- Legislative Branch (since 1990)

Presidents:
_____
_____
_____
_____
_____

Chief Justices of the Supreme Court:
_____
_____
_____
_____

Senators:
_____
_____
_____
_____
_____

Representatives:
_____
_____
_____
_____
_____
_____
_____

On a separate piece of paper, write a two or three sentence paragraph telling how the national government of the United States serves people in our state.

© Scott Foresman

Learning About Your State and Community

Name _____ Date _____

Who Governs Our State?

The capitol building houses the offices of those who govern our state. What does the capitol building in our state look like? Draw a picture of the front of our state capitol in the space below.

Complete the statements about our state government. If necessary, use resources such as an encyclopedia or state-fact book.

1 The capital city of our state is _____.

2 The name of our governor is _____.

3 The governor is elected for _____ years.

4 The governor is responsible for _____.

5 The bodies of our state legislature are called the _____ and the _____.

6 The legislature is responsible for _____.

7 The judicial branch of our state includes the _____ court and the _____ court.

8 Judges are responsible for _____.

20

Learning About Your State and Community

© Scott Foresman

Name _____ Date _____

The Governor of Our State

Use the Internet or other resources in the library to learn about the governor of our state. Write a paragraph introducing him or her. Tell what part of the state the governor calls home, what other jobs the governor has held, some information about the governor's family, and any other interesting information that you can find.

_____
_____
_____
_____
_____
_____
_____

Find an article about the governor of our state on the Internet or in a newspaper or news magazine. Copy the headline. Name the site or publication in which the article appeared. Give the publication's date.

_____
_____
_____
_____

Suppose you want to be the governor of our state someday. What skills do you think you will need to develop? Use the space below and the back of this page to write a brief paragraph about the steps you would take to become a governor.

_____
_____
_____
_____
_____
_____

Learning About Your State and Community

21

Name _____ Date _____

The State Legislature

Use references such as a library to find information about a state legislator. Complete the address card with the information.

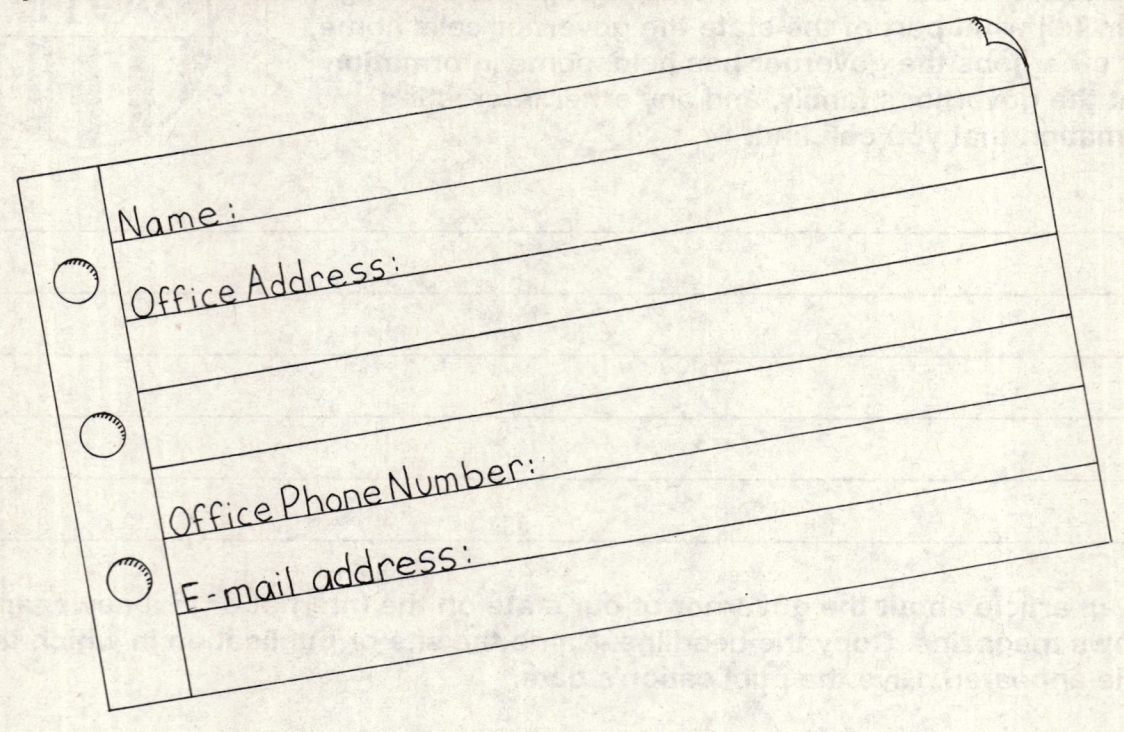

```
Name:
Office Address:


Office Phone Number:
E-mail address:
```

Suppose you could be a member of the state legislature. What kind of new law would you try to make? What problem would the law solve? Complete the diagram below.

Problem	Solution
	Law:

22   Learning About Your State and Community

Name _____ Date _____

The Judicial Branch

The judicial branch of our state government consists of its courts. Use your research skills to find out the name of the court in our state that should hear each case. Complete the chart below.

Case	Court that should hear the case
A state law is not allowed under the state constitution.	
A citizen is accused of burglary.	
A motorist is accused of speeding.	

Find out how a person becomes a judge in our state. What qualities do you think a judge should have?

_____
_____
_____
_____
_____
_____
_____
_____
_____
_____
_____
_____

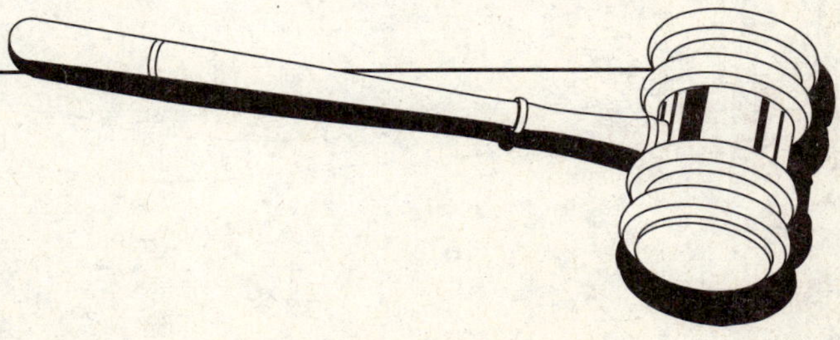

Learning About Your State and Community

Name _____   Date _____

Education

One important service that the state government provides is education. Education can be very expensive. Use your research skills to find out about our state's educational system and answer the questions.

How much did our state spend last year on education? _____

Where does the state get the money to spend on education? _____
_____

How many students attended public schools in our state last year? _____

What percentage of students in our state go to college each year? _____

Name some colleges and universities in our state. _____
_____

Going to school and getting an education is important. How will it help you prepare for the future? In what ways does our state help with your education? Write a brief paragraph that answers these questions.

_____
_____
_____
_____
_____
_____
_____
_____
_____

24

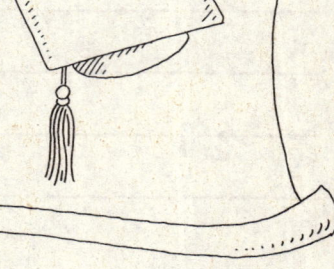

Learning About Your State and Community

Name _____   Date _____

Industries and the Economy

Industries contribute to our state's economy in many ways. Look in an almanac or an encyclopedia to complete the sentences.

The crops grown in our state include _____
_____.

The products manufactured in our state include _____
_____.

The natural resources that contribute to our state's economy are _____
_____.

Among the large companies that employ people in the state are _____
_____.

Examples of service jobs, or jobs that people do for others, in our

state include _____

_____

_____.

Find out about the largest industry in our state. Write about how it contributes to life in our state. When did it start? What are its products? How many people work in that industry? In what city or cities is it located? How much money does it bring to the state yearly?

_____
_____
_____
_____
_____

Learning About Your State and Community

25

Name _____   Date _____

State Celebrations

What annual celebrations in our state honor state events or people? What festivals are held at different times of the year? Use your research skills to find out. Complete the idea web below about one celebration that you think is interesting.

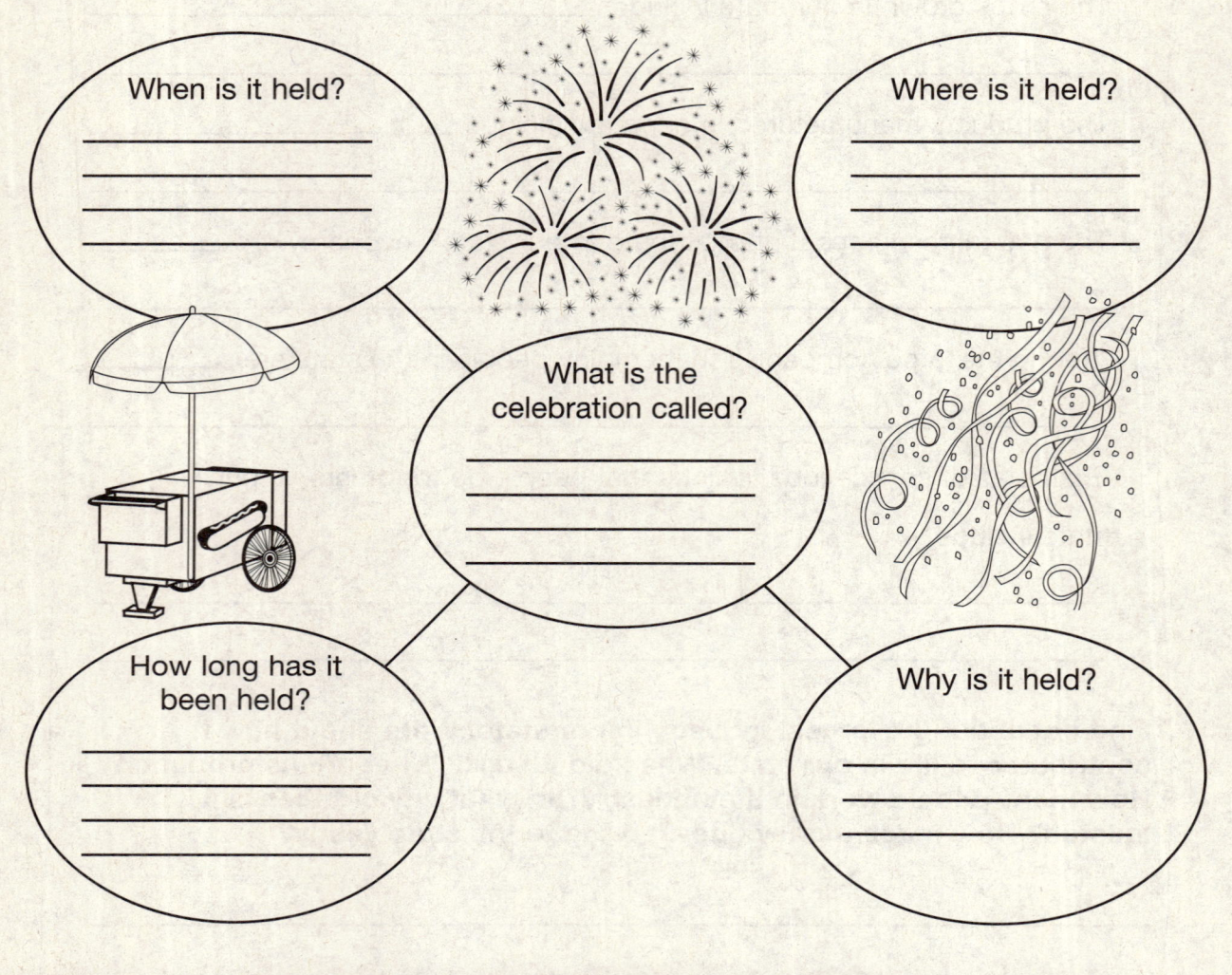

- When is it held? _____
- Where is it held? _____
- What is the celebration called? _____
- How long has it been held? _____
- Why is it held? _____

What is your favorite state celebration? Write a brief paragraph describing the event.

_____
_____
_____

Name _____ Date _____

Cultural Resources

States are proud of their cultural resources. Listed in the table below are different types of cultural resources. Name an example of each resource that is available in or near your community.

Cultural Resources	Name
Museum or Historical Society	
Library	
Movie Theater	
Sports Arena	
Stage for Live Performances	
Park	

Complete the sentences below about the cultural resources in our state.

MUSEUM of ART ADMIT ONE

One state museum is called _____.

Among the exhibits in the museum are _____

_____.

One of our sports teams is called _____.

They play at the _____.

When tourists come to our state, they like to see _____

_____

Another attraction is the _____

Learning About Your State and Community

27

Name _____ Date _____

Arts and Crafts

Use an almanac, an encyclopedia, the Internet, or other sources to find out about artists born in our state. What kind of art have they created? Use the information you find to fill in the chart.

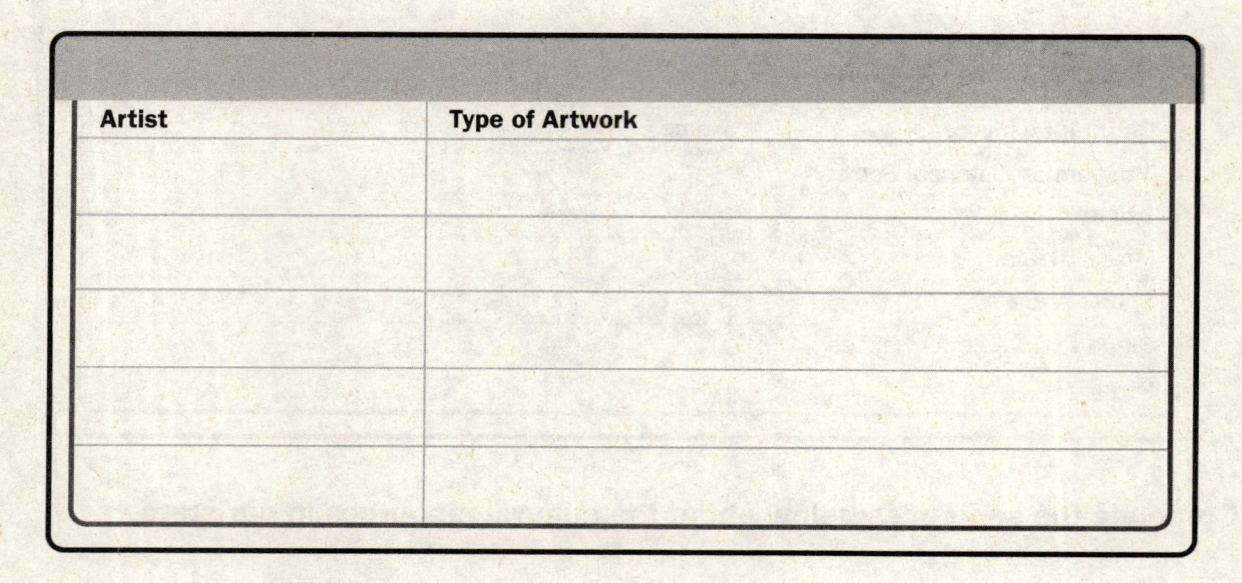

Artist	Type of Artwork

Suppose you were one of the artists assigned to design a new logo for our state. What would your idea for a logo look like? Sketch the logo in the circle. Then write a brief paragraph on the back of this page explaining your design.

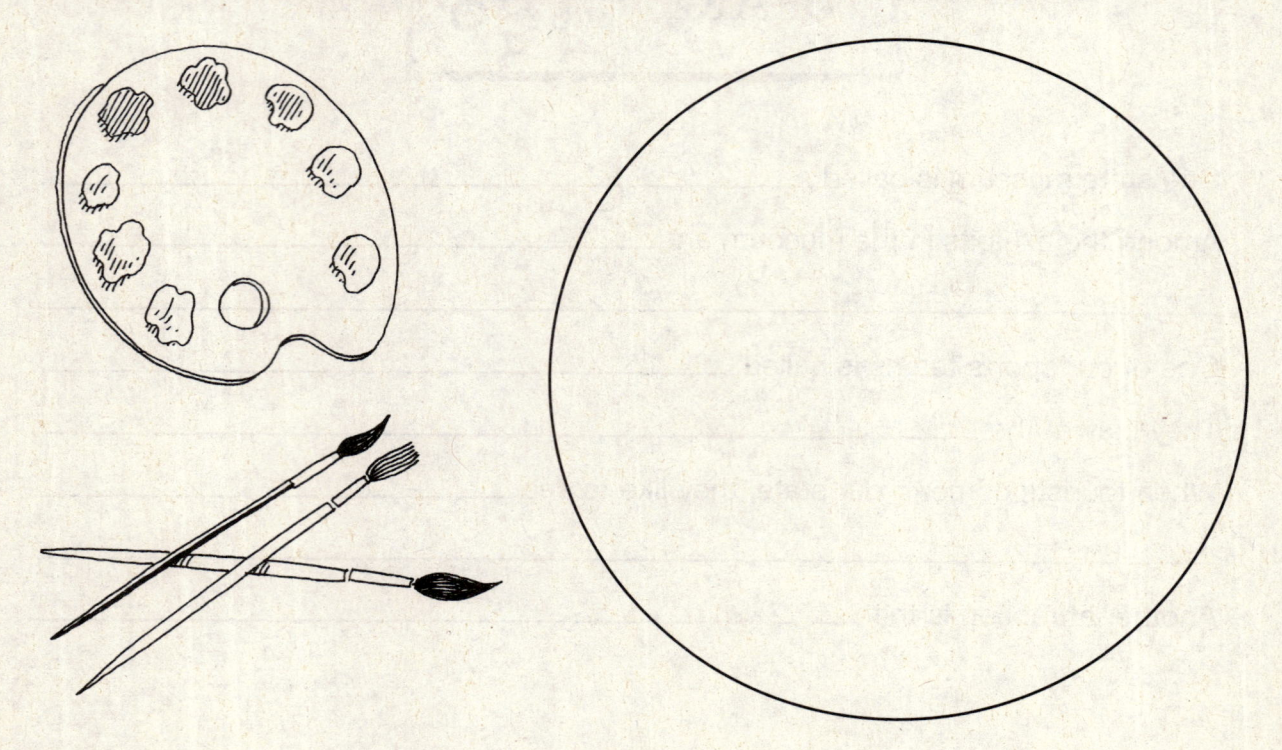

28

Learning About Your State and Community

Name _____ Date _____

Literature

Find books about our state. On each of the cards below, complete the information for three of the books you found.

Title: _____
Author: _____
Subject: _____
_____
_____
_____

Title: _____
Author: _____
Subject: _____
_____
_____
_____

Title: _____
Author: _____
Subject: _____
_____
_____
_____

Suppose you are writing a book about our state. Write a table of contents that shows the chapter titles you will use in your book. Use the back side of this paper if you need more room.

_____
_____
_____
_____
_____
_____
_____

© Scott Foresman

Learning About Your State and Community

Name _____ Date _____

Sports

Many opportunities exist in our state to take part in outdoor activities or to watch sports events. Based on what you know, complete the following sentences.

A popular sports activity in our state is _____.

People like it because _____
_____

A favorite sports team in our state is _____,

which plays _____.

In each of the smaller boxes, write the name of a famous athlete from our state to support the main idea.

Main idea: Our state has produced a number of well-known athletes.

30 Learning About Your State and Community

Name _____ Date _____

Getting Around Our State

How easy is it to get around our state? Use what you know and your research skills to answer these questions about transportation.

Choose another community in our state. What different kinds of transportation can you use to get from your community to that community? _____
_____

What interstate highways pass through our state? _____
_____

Where is a major airport located in our state? _____

What public transportation systems, if any, are available in cities in our state? _____
_____

How do most students in your community get to school?
_____

Suppose you are a bus driver for a group of tourists visiting our state. Which roads would you choose to take them to a historical site? Describe what the tourists would see on the way.

_____
_____
_____
_____
_____
_____

Learning About Your State and Community

Name _____ Date _____

Places to Visit

There are many kinds of places a tourist can visit in our state. Fill in the spaces in the table with examples.

Kind of Place	Examples
Natural Wonders	
Early Historical Sites	
Entertainment/Recreational Sites	
City Sites	

Use what you know about the places to visit in our state to create a brochure that will invite people to see various attractions. Use the spaces in the brochure below or create a brochure on a separate sheet of paper.

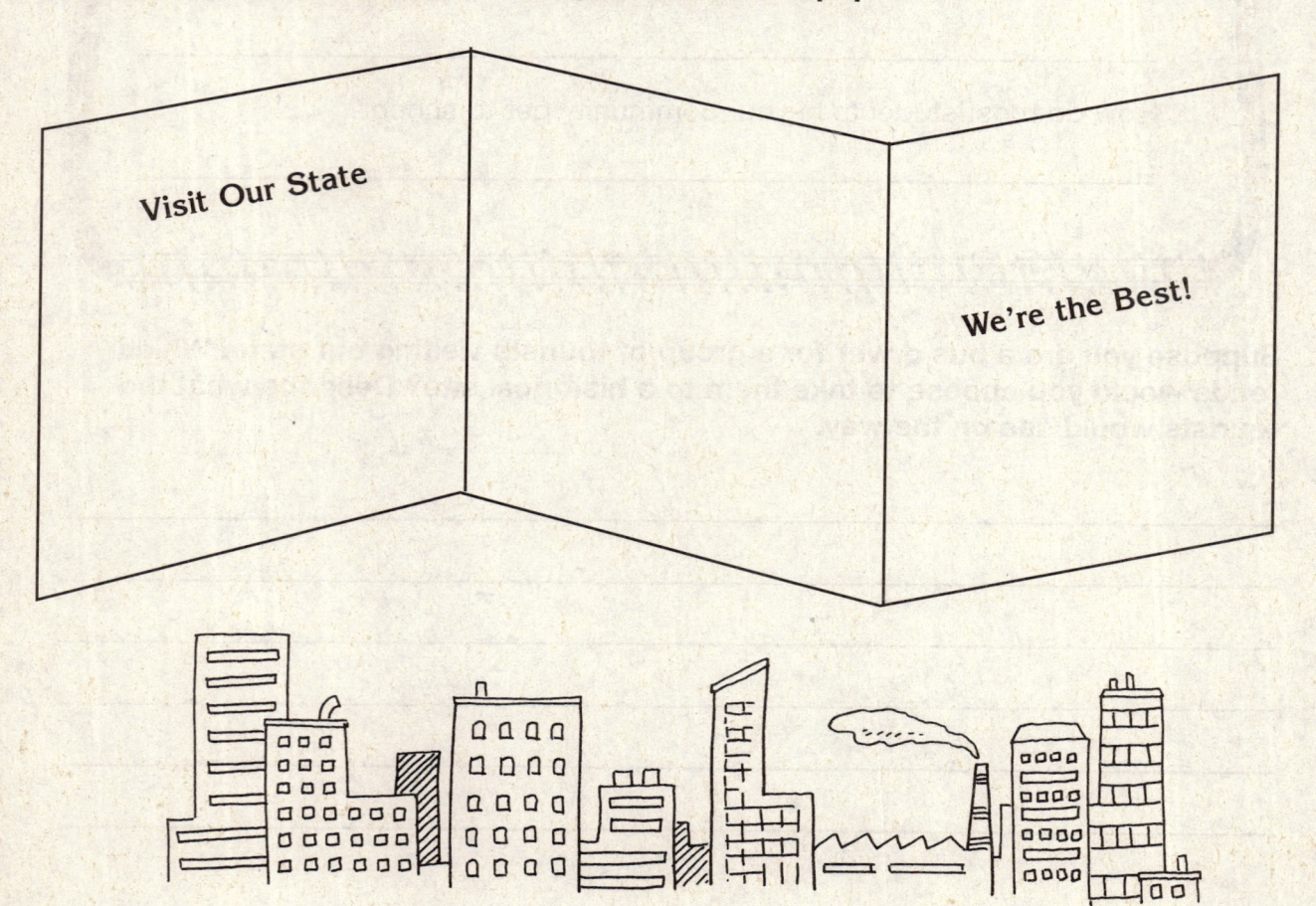

Visit Our State

We're the Best!

32

Learning About Your State and Community

Name _____ Date _____

Something to Write Home About

Suppose that you are visiting our state for the first time. Fill out the postcard below to send home. Describe what you like about the state and some of your favorite places.

All states have their own motto. Write our state motto below. Then tell what idea the motto wants people to know about our state.

_____
_____
_____
_____
_____
_____

Learning About Your State and Community 33

Name _____ Date _____

State Symbols

All states have their own symbols. Use what you have learned and your research skills to draw the symbols of our state. Use correct colors.

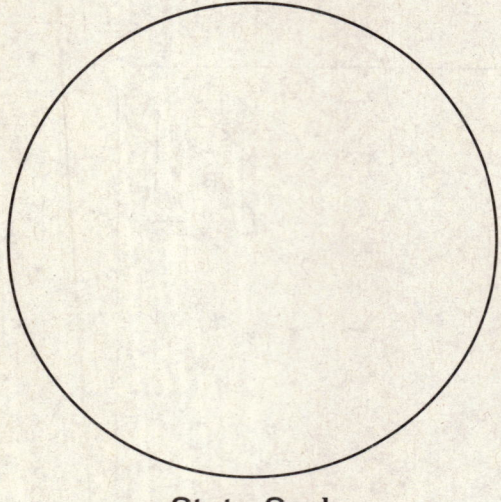

State Seal

State Flag

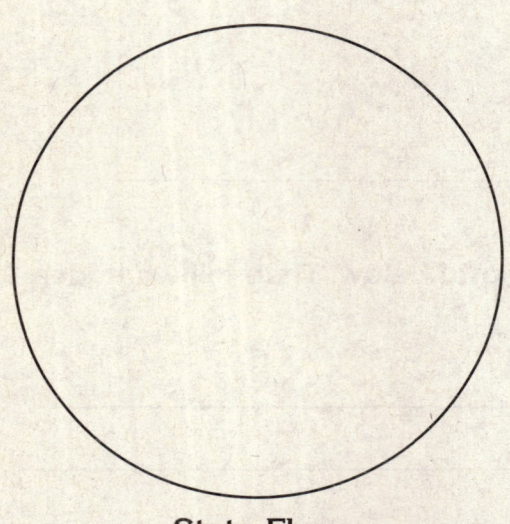

State Flower

State Bird

Name other symbols for our state on the back of this page.

34

Learning About Your State and Community

Name _____ Date _____

Cities and Towns

Every state has cities and towns. Look at a state map or an atlas. Then fill in the blanks to complete the information about the cities and towns in our state.

The biggest city in our state is _____.

One of the smallest towns in our state is _____.

The most famous city or town in our state is probably _____.

Every tourist should visit the city or town of _____

because _____.

_____ is the unusual name of a city or town in our state.

Write about which town or city in our state is your favorite and tell why you like it.

_____
_____
_____
_____
_____
_____

© Scott Foresman

Learning About Your State and Community

35

Name _____ Date _____

Make a Map of Your Community

Use the space below to make a map of your community. Your community may be a small town. It may be a neighborhood in a large city. If you live outside a town or city, it may cover a large area of a countryside. Show the places people go, such as the post office, school, library, stores, and landmarks. Label these features clearly so that others could use your map to find their way around your community. Keep your map for future use.

- Post Office
- Hospital
- Restaurant
- School
- Store

Learning About Your State and Community

Name _____ Date _____

Your Local Government

Make Who's Who cards about up to four elected officials in your local government. In the boxes below, write each person's name. Then list the person's job title, term of office, and main duties. Use different resources, if necessary.

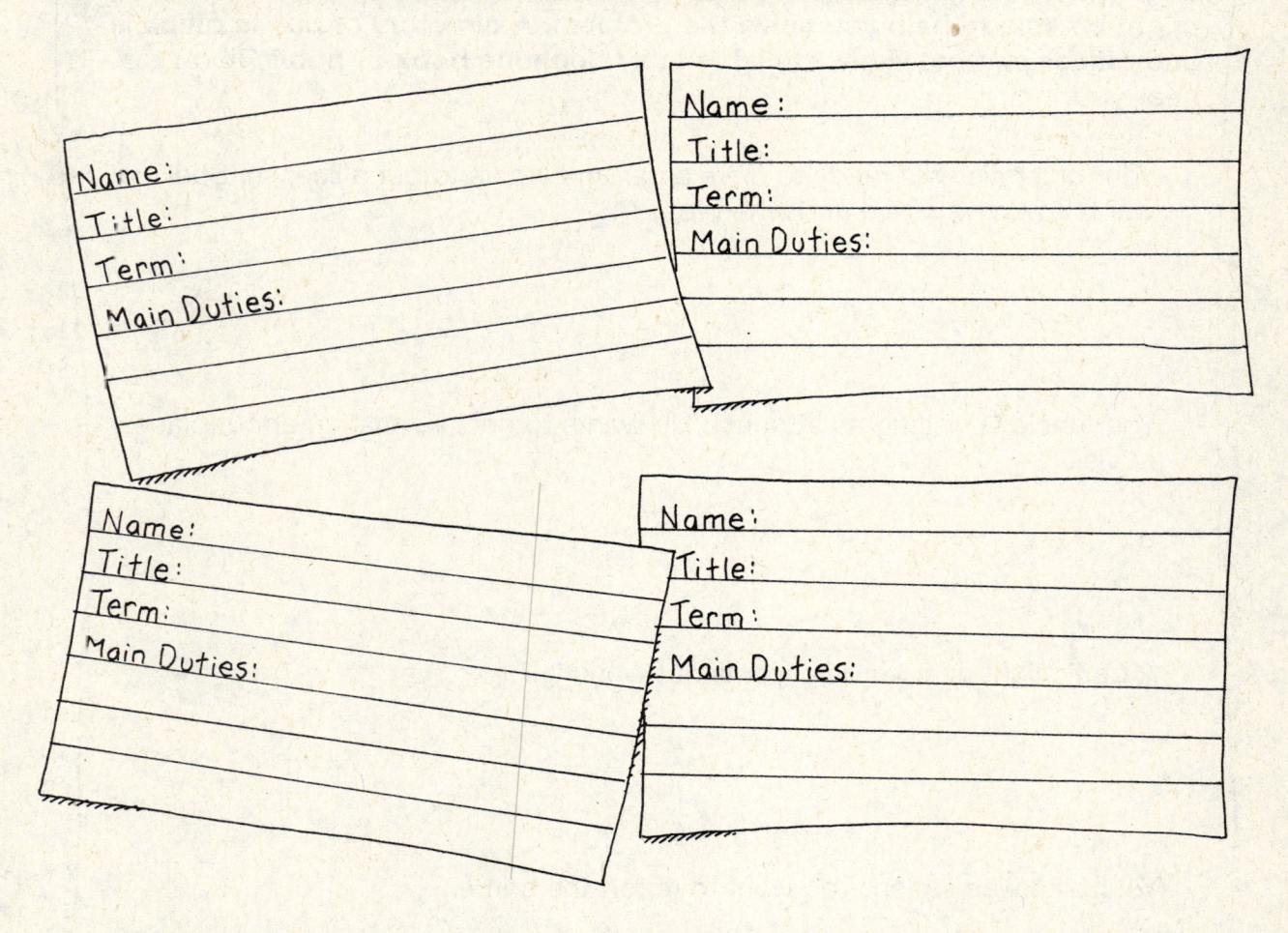

```
Name:
Title:
Term:
Main Duties:
```

```
Name:
Title:
Term:
Main Duties:
```

```
Name:
Title:
Term:
Main Duties:
```

```
Name:
Title:
Term:
Main Duties:
```

In each of the smaller boxes, write a factual detail that supports the conclusion.

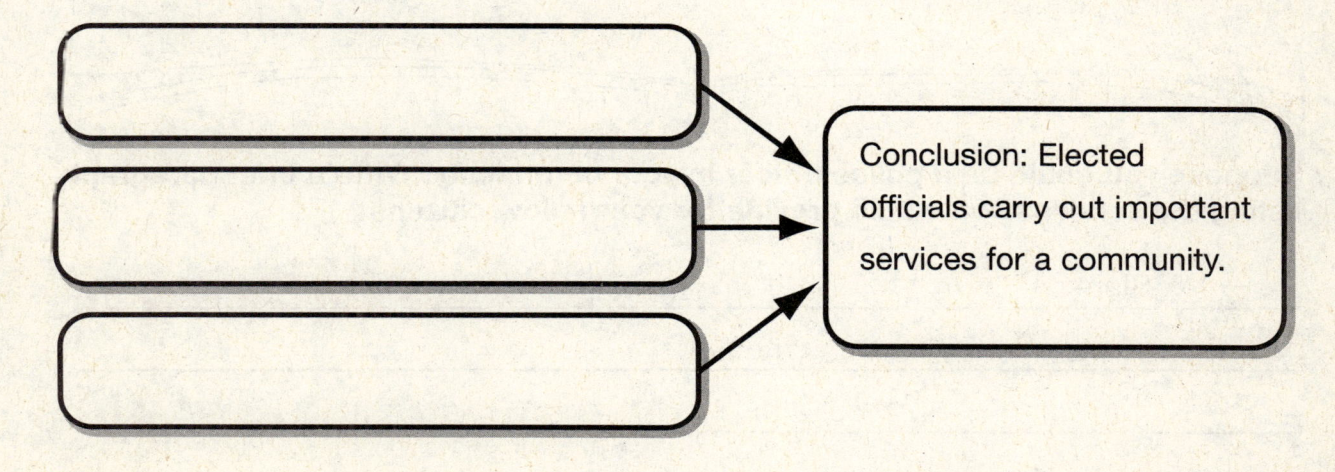

Conclusion: Elected officials carry out important services for a community.

© Scott Foresman

Learning About Your State and Community

37

Name _____   Date _____

Getting the Help You Need

Why might you need to contact a government office? For each problem description, write the name and address of the office or person who might be able to help you solve the problem. A directory of public officials and offices is most likely available in a telephone book or public library near you.

Your older sister is ready to drive a car and wants to get a license. She wants to know where and when to go.

Your uncle is visiting as a tourist. He wants to get information about places to visit.

A traffic light near your school is not working.

Your bike was stolen. You want to report the crime.

Suppose you could be a police officer in your community. Write a brief paragraph listing the services you would provide for your fellow citizens.

_____
_____
_____
_____

38   Learning About Your State and Community

Name _____ Date _____

Important People from Your Community

Work with a group of classmates. Name three people who have made a difference in your community's history. Ask your school librarian to suggest resources. Fill in the information indicated in the table below. Choose different kinds of people, such as community leaders, authors, or teachers.

Name   Accomplishments
_____   _____
_____   _____
_____   _____

Would you like to be a famous and honored person in your community? What contributions would you like to make? Complete the award sheet about you as a locally famous person.

I, _____, contributed to my community in these ways:

_____
_____
_____
_____
_____
_____
_____

Learning About Your State and Community

Name _____ Date _____

Touring Your Town or City

Use the town or city map you made to plan a walking tour for a visitor. Take the visitor to as many of the interesting places in your town or city as can be seen in a day. Fill in the schedule below.

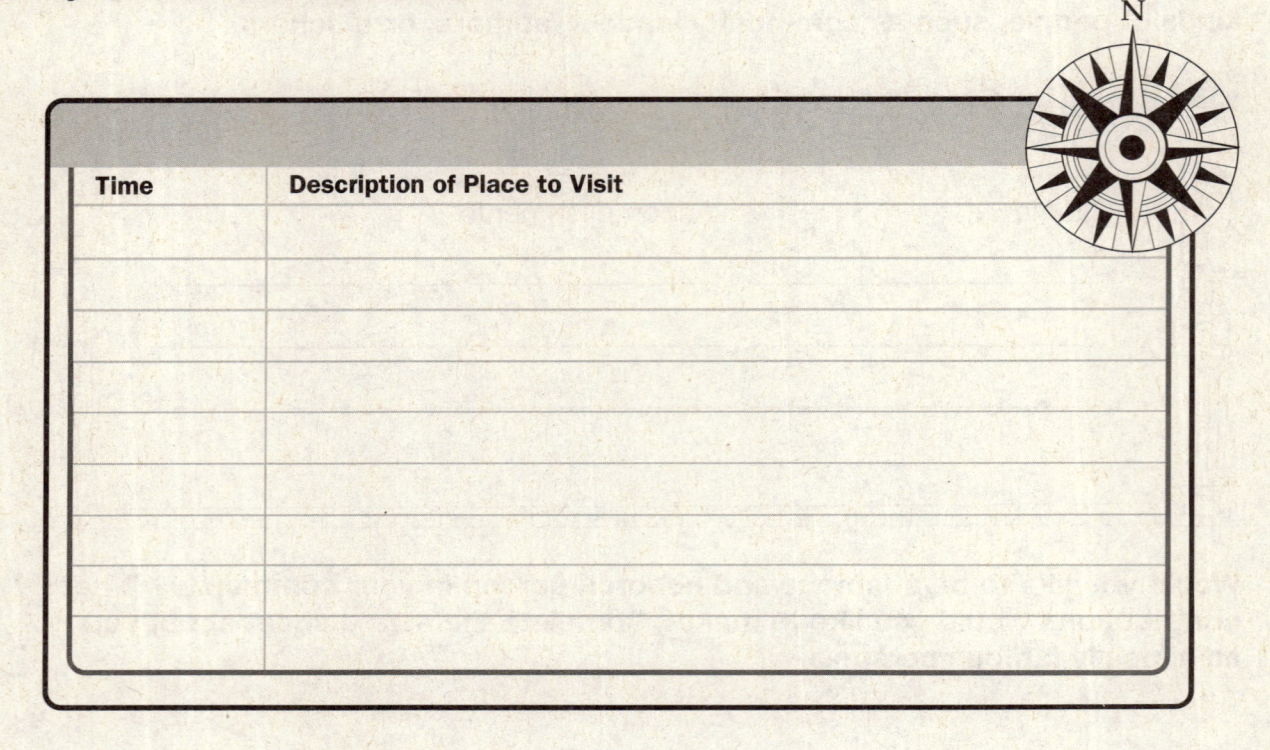

Time	Description of Place to Visit

Tell a visitor to go to a restaurant or store leaving from your school. Using a map of your community, write specific directions by filling in the blanks.

To get to _____, follow these directions:

From the front of my school, turn _____.

Then _____.

Next _____

_____.

Finally _____.

Name _____ Date _____

Community Landmark

Create a poster about a landmark in your community. Draw a picture of it in the space below and tell why the landmark is important on the lines at the bottom.

_____
_____
_____

Learning About Your State and Community

41

Name _____ Date _____

Your Community: Past and Future

What was life like in your community 50 years ago? Ask someone who lived in your community then. Based on your conversation, answer the questions.

What work did most people do?
_____
_____

How did people get to and from work? _____
_____

Where did most people live? _____

What did people do when they wanted to relax and have fun? _____
_____

To what places did they take visitors? _____
_____

What was school like in this community 50 years ago? _____
_____

What about this community has changed the most? _____
_____

Predict what life in your community will be like 50 years from now. Write a brief paragraph about your community's future.

_____
_____
_____
_____
_____
_____
_____

42   LEARNING ABOUT YOUR STATE AND COMMUNITY

Name _____ Date _____

Our State and Your Community at a Glance

Summarize what you have learned about our state and your community. Fill in the blanks with the correct information.

State name: _____ Postal abbreviation: _____

Origin of state name: _____

State motto: _____ State capital: _____

State nickname: _____

Date of statehood: _____

Population: _____ Rank in nation: _____

Land area: _____ Rank in nation: _____

Names of major waterways and/or landforms: _____
_____

My community: _____

When my community was founded: _____

Population of my community: _____

Write an interesting fact about our state and an interesting fact about your community on the back of this page.

LEARNING ABOUT YOUR STATE AND COMMUNITY

43

Name _____ Date _____

Community Hero

If you had to choose someone who contributes a lot to your community, who would it be? Think of a person who deserves a Certificate of Appreciation for what he or she does. On the certificate below, write the name of the person and say why you think that person deserves the certificate. You may give that person the certificate if you wish.

CERTIFICATE OF APPRECIATION

This certificate is presented to

_____

in appreciation for these contributions to our community:

_____
_____
_____
_____
_____
_____
_____
_____

Learning About Your State and Community